FOREWORD BY KECIA LOTEZ

Your Guide to Become a Wife Whose Prayers Move Mountains

WIFE
PRAY
WIN

Wife Pray Win

*Your Guide to Become a Wife Whose
Prayers Move Mountains*

YOLANDA LEWIS

Extreme Overflow Publishing
Dacula, GA
USA

Published by Extreme Overflow Publishing
A Division of Extreme Overflow Enterprises, Inc
Dacula, Georgia 30019
www.extremeoverflow.com

Photo Credit: www.123rf.com
Library of Congress Cataloging-Publication
Data is available for this title.
ISBN: 978-0-9989351-7-1

Printed in the United States of America

FOREWORD

Eve, don't eat the forbidden fruit!
Sarah, don't give another woman to your husband!
Jezebel don't usurp your husband's authority!

In each of these situations, all three women were not cognizant of the consequences their decisions would have on their marriage. As women, we are prone to the temptations of this world. Sometimes, too easily, we can be persuaded by our natural eyes for what appears to be the good, pleasing, and desirable way to make one wise. This is very real for some of us and can lead to a trap of destruction in a marriage.

Marriage is a sacred oath. Upholding the marital vows, acknowledged before God, is our obligation to the union. In the blessed union of marriage, the two become one flesh. There is no longer a, "you" or "I" in the relationship. It now becomes "us" for the purpose of fulfilling designed order on earth. As a wife, we play a critical role in our husband's life. The key is to understand and know what that role is in order to fulfill our God-designed purpose.

When it comes to marriage, our past experiences will either be a hindrance or become a reference point for managing marital challenges. The Bible asks, "Can two walk together unless they are agreed?" (Amos 3:3 NKJV). In a covenant marriage, the two shall become one flesh in deed, choice, and action. If one partner transgresses, both are held responsible because you are in a joint partnership, as one flesh. Therefore, it will be necessary, as a wife, to continually pray and intercede for deliverance, healing, and restoration for the marriage union to be made whole by God.

Becoming one unit, united on all fronts

establishes a foundation of strength, trust, obedience, and love that can overcome any test, trial, or tribulation. In life, we will have many tests and obstacles to overcome. The key is to understand that the purpose of the test is to strengthen faith and commitment to each other and to God. As we trust His guidance for the outcome, we can depend on God to see us through.

Words have the power to create or destroy life. What we speak over our marriages has a lasting effect on our life trajectory. Likewise, trials and tribulations can be viewed as blessings if we look at them from the right perspective. There are numerous things and situations we can complain about in a relationship. But a great prescription for complaining is prayer. Speaking words of affirmation will impart purpose and destiny in our marriages. Regardless of the circumstance or situation, we will find that God is always with us.

His favor, grace, and mercy will keep us as we persevere and remain the course despite whatever is presented before us. The situation in and of itself may not be ideal, but knowing the significance is vital. Having a consistent prayer life will change your perception of your marriage, and relieve you from carrying the burden alone.

Because we live in an unsettling and chaotic world, it is important for wives to take position and stance as prayer warriors. We are to pray without ceasing and not lose heart. In the world of sports, each player must know the position they play. Their awareness of the purpose and power in their position maintains unity, cohesion, homogeneity, and structure. It helps to position the team for a successful outcome through a planned strategy. By knowing our position as wives, we are able to play it well, sow seeds of blessings, and help others in the process.

As a licensed social worker who performs marriage counseling, it is most important to maintain a victorious marriage by, persevering through the process, respecting the process, accepting the process, and yielding to the process (of growth). We are living in the days where people are watching and emulating others and not focusing on their own lives. In these situations, it can be easy to lose focus on what's important. In order to be prepared for what is to come, as wives we must pray and watch for the signs of the times. In this season, something special is in the making. Everything is being made new. Listen and pay attention to the challenges at hand. They will uncover the gift within and release untapped energy and ability to help you build a great marriage.

Mrs. Yolanda Lewis, renowned author, publisher, entrepreneur, coach, mentor, wife, and mother, is on time with this book, "Wife. Pray. Win." Her ability to write this book comes from a wealth of knowledge and firsthand experience. She is a campaigner for successful marriages.

My first encounter with Yolanda was over 20 years ago in the financial industry. She was ambitious and eager to learn, so I hired her to participate in an avant-garde training program for developing young leaders. As a natural leader, Yolanda excelled at every challenge set before her. Since that time, Yolanda has unceasingly demonstrated determination, drive, and tenacity to succeed in life, which has charted her course in the professional world. Her accomplished dreams and aspirations are an encouragement for others to know that opportunities in life are limitless.

This book is a must-read for all women, regardless of your marital status. As a powerful weapon, this book can be used to revolutionize any marital relationship, at any season of life. It is a tool to help prepare for marriage as well. The main premise of this book is to inspire the marriage union to be fruitful, prosperous, and victorious through prayer. Praying over every evil force lurking in the shadows to discourage and disrupt perfect matrimony.

It's easy to become overly consumed with particular situations or circumstances in our lives. But through it all, we must not forget what is most important. Giving of oneself through prayer requires loving each other unconditionally, as well as following instructions that may go against our way of thinking or doing things. The anecdote to avoid demise is to stay in tune with the inner voice (within). Pray consistently. Follow the instructions, guidance, and warnings from the inner promptings of faith. These promptings are given for our protection. God always has your best interest in mind. The key to mastering this level of prayer is to submit and believe that all things are possible and will work together for the good. Do what is needed regardless of what others may say or think. Seek God for a greater understanding. At the appropriate times, it will help with making the right decision. The book, "Wife. Pray. Win." was written for such a time as this.

Kecia Lopes, LGSW

Table of Contents

INTRODUCTION

Nothing can be restored if it is not first broken.

Love is a fruit of marriage. Your relationship will be hanging on by a thread if love is the only reason why your marriage exists. Many confuse the expression of love as the totality of what a marital relationship should be established by. However, love is only one aspect of a good marriage. Love is a must have, but not the only have in your relationship. The misunderstanding of this concept is where the conflict begins.

Yesterday's big argument, last week's mis-understanding, and tomorrow's foul play can disintegrate the trust you once had for your partner. Love will conquer all yet love alone won't fix a thing. When trust is broken, unaddressed, or festered it grows frustration and will create division within the marital relationship. In this place of division, it won't be long before you find your marriage officially "on the rocks."

Since women are natural bearers of pain, we have a pretty high tolerance for it. The problem in being able to take a lot of pain causes conflict when pain gives permission to express itself in an unhealthy way. Unhealthy behavior in a marriage looks nothing like love. It is violent, self-centered, and intentionally hurtful at best. The unhealthy expression of pain is a professional at tricking you into thinking, "I got it." It forces you beyond the limits of what love is supposed to represent. When in reality you just want to be free from the angst being married to who my grandma would call, "Skeebo," is causing you. In those moments, you just want peace. In those moments, love is silent and sometimes seems invisible, even when it is present. Some women try to fulfill this longing for real love, with the replacement of another person;

a strategy that never works.

Before getting married, women tend to scour the earth for love without knowing what love means to them. Without knowing the type of love they require and expect, women end up married and dissatisfied. Easily the marriage is stained with contempt. Without boundaries, this "love" spreads into every area of your relationship, confusing sound judgment, diminishing value, and purpose. Before you know it, you are lost in a sea of relational toxicity, mislabeled as love. You then fantasize about the ways you can escape the current, even though you're already married. Divorce is the option that always presents the strongest case for being the answer. However, it is not the only answer. There is another way. There is prayer.

Sometimes the advice of "just pray," sounds

cliche. Sure, you've prayed before. But let me tell you why many prayers do not produce change. Prayer cannot be used as witchcraft. Prayer witchcraft is any prayer used to manipulate a person or a situation for selfish gain. Prayers prayed in an attempt to manipulate may sound innocent and or even spiritual. But there is no form of manipulation from God. There is a huge difference in praying prayers that produce change verses praying prayers that cast or request spell work and release what turns into generational curses. To know how to pray is to know how to stand in authority as a chosen oracle of God's blessed will. There is a divine power bestowed upon you when you become a wife. That power is often lost in love. Every woman needs to know their power and operate in it, in order to positively charge a healthy marital environment or a restored marital relationship.

Marriage is by nature a partnership to build. Through problem-solving together, expanding resources together, and creating together, the marital relationship grows. It improves. Love and even sex are just the mere expressions of how these building blocks of legacy are achieved. Couples in today's modern society are in need of re-education of what marriage is so that husbands and wives can create the lives God intended through their partnership.

We're human and are prone to get lost along the way. We need guidance. We need God. We need prayer. Prayer is the exhibition of hope in a situation or circumstance that is contrary to God's best for your life and the life of your partner, as one. As wives, we pray to satisfy God's will on the earth, through the relationship of marriage.

Through hard lessons, doubt, and tears I

learned that prayer is real. It works and changes things, people, perception, and expectation. There were times in my marriage where I prayed for my husband and didn't see answers until years later. However, God was always working. He always had his hand on my nontraditional relationship. While I prayed and sometimes felt dismayed, God was sending my husband all types of messages in all types of ways. He was giving him direction, purpose, and the like throughout our marriage. Most of them I didn't see manifest until after the fact. Essentially, the power in my role as a wife was most imminent when I got down on my knees and prayed for my husband for real. Change then manifested when my belief in what God was going to do with our brokenness aligned with His will.

Broken is a great place to begin restoration. Broken is a great place to start building again. Perhaps you've been in a marital relationship that's felt sour for some time now. Maybe you've been in a marriage and prayed for change you have yet to see. You may have even begged for God's hand to move but things seem like they will never change. Matter of fact, they may even seem like the more you pray the worse things get. I've been there. I'm here to tell you there is truth to be found and hope to be gained. Prayer has the power to change things no one else can.

Throughout this book, you will explore the power of prayer as a wife. You'll learn how to find hope again in prayer, and use prayer effectively, no matter what your current situation appears to be. By the end of this book, you will know that it's never too late to restore, repair, and enjoy true relationship with your husband. To win in the married life, takes change. That change has to start with you and must begin today.

WIFE

"He who finds a wife,

finds a good thing and obtains favor from God."

Psalm 18:22

Chapter 1
Fix, Raise, Grow

"I can't fix you. I'm just your wife."

I've heard women say you can grow your man. They say you can train him to be the kind of man you want. These truths have no power. If you want a powerless relationship, go ahead. Build a man.

In building your own man, you will find that there is only one problem. Building your own man gets in the way of God's design, His intention for your relationship. It disrespects God's plan and robs essentiality from the purpose you were brought together to accomplish. All of your efforts to grow a man will fall out of alignment with God's divine appointment for you as his destined help mate. In other words, the man you try to grow, won't ever become the man you were made to build with. Only God knows what you and your husband needs are with one another, which cannot be manmade.

When you were joined together in holy matrimony before witnesses and angels, something deeper than "I do," happened. There was a spiritual electricity transferred between the two of you. Energies bounced, angels danced, and heaven rejoiced when you both stood in agreement to commit your lives before God, to one another. There is no argument in hell that can change that.

My husband and I knew each other from church first. On occasion, his grandmother made him go. By high school, we were attending the same school. I saw him in the hallways and after school in the community. He was one of the cool and very handsome kids. I wasn't what some would call, "cool" at all. Actually, I went to school on senior skip day! See, not cool. But in my own way, I was full of life and fun.

After graduation, we met again two years into my college career. At the time, I had no idea of how to pay for school and had tapped out of resources to be able to go further. I needed a new plan. My best friend was heading off to the military. She too didn't have money for college. Coming from a military family, the idea didn't sound half bad as an option for myself. The problem was, I started dating a guy from high school whom I really liked. We had only dated for a few months.

However, there wasn't a day that went by where we didn't hang out. But I had decided. I needed to finish school. My parents needed me to repay my student loans. I had to find a way to pay them back and finish school. I didn't mind serving in the military, I just needed confirmation that I was going in the right direction. I asked my boyfriend about us. While he was officially my boyfriend, I wasn't sure if he was serious about seeing someone, let alone build a life together. I asked him the infamous question of, "what are we?" To which he replied, "You know we're just chillin.'" That was the answer I needed. There was no way I was going to tell him that I was really feeling him. He was handsome, brilliant, worked three jobs and had his own car when we met. Pride wouldn't let me admit to him how I felt. I decided to enjoy things while they lasted knowing that soon I'd be moving on.

The next day I enlisted in the military. Like normal, my boyfriend picked me up from the train station. We greeted each other with pleasantries. Nothing new. He smelled so good. He got off of work earlier than I did and had time to pick me up, shower fresh. He asked me how my day was and I told him that I signed up for the military and would be leaving soon. Without hesitation, he stopped the car in the middle of traffic and turned and looked me in my eyes to say, "You're not going anywhere without me." No cars honked, no one skidded off. It was as if time itself stopped. We've been together ever since.

The next day he enlisted. The weeks following his proclamation we used his grandmothers green notebook to start drawing out our life. We didn't discuss that we were going to do this, we just did. It was an instant knee-jerk reaction of commitment. The spiritual and magnetic connection we shared inspired him to dream, inspired him to see and inspired him to write down a vision that we together would follow. We didn't know it until later, but we actually drew our first house. We didn't have it built. The vision we had for our house was almost as if we knew the builder. Eight years later our vision manifested and we bought our first home.

I didn't grow him. We were made for each other.

There is tremendous authority when women take their rightful place as wife. Too often women settle in their marriage living in only half of their power. I too was guilty of living in only half of my power as a wife. Within those eight years, between stopping traffic and buying a house, we struggled. We were challenged in every way possible. Our vision was shaken, promises broken, and hearts made sensitive with unbearable truth. We were growing up and learning so many things about ourselves. To find that there were some things we didn't like. For years I stood in the way of my husband's maturation process. Unintentionally, I blocked his release while also blocking my own freedom. I spent a lot of energy trying to fix things; him, me, and us. I thought I was being loyal to God and our marriage by the demonstration of my commitment by throwing myself on the train tracks of lessons sometimes just he was supposed to learn. In the name of love, I strained the call on both of our lives.

The reality is you can't raise, fix or grow your man. He's already grown and if he's not, only God can change you both. Whatever he was supposed to learn and didn't, is not for you to show him. It is not for your to fix. His lessons, just like yours are between him and God. You're

Wife Pray Win

only assigned to be his wife.

Chapter 2

The Upgrade

"I'm here to help. By nature, I upgrade you."

As a wife, you are an equal to your husband. Egoism and culture have tainted and in many cases have caused people to lose sight of the value God intended for the role of a wife in the marital relationship. Every skill, every gift, every talent is designed to help your husband satisfy the vision God entrusted to him. The vision God is expecting your union to fulfill. Help is not a negative word. You have the best seat in the house as your husbands help meet. You, your style, your flavor, and your anointing are the missing pieces he needs to execute the vision at hand. You can see things he can't. You can feel things he misses. You are needed in the marital journey toward purpose. It could be, that God wanted you to start that business first so that it could be a set up for your husband's business later. Think union minded. As a wife, you serve in part. Part of your vision is a part of his vision, all for God's glory. Don't get distracted by the details. Don't be emotionally attached to the way things may come about. The way you think it should be is not the only way it can happen. God is infinite in his power and strategic in his intention. He knows what he's doing. Trust the direction. As a winning wife, the challenge is to be open to understanding that God's grace is sufficient. You with all that you bring to the table, beyond hips and lipstick, help birth the vision to fruition. You are the key to the visions ignition. He needs you, just as much as you need him. As it has been said, you can be a movement by yourself but you are a force to be reckoned with when you move together. Meaning, if you try to use your key in any other ignition, with any other person than the man God aligned to be your husband, the vision will never get started. For this reason, the man who you call your husband is divinely meant to be your life building partner whether you see it or not.

I can recall so many times my husband had ideas of starting businesses. Great ideas. However, we had gotten to a place in our relationship where I couldn't see past the bills that were due and the financial need of the family. I was distracted by responsibility. Among other things, I neglected to give my husband the encouragement he needed to fulfill the vision(s) God had entrusted him to accomplish. My key was not in the ignition of his vision. Which meant my business skills and financial acumen weren't being utilized for their intended purposes. As a result, it left my husband searching for purpose he already had. Subsequently leaving me searching for vision to fulfill.

It was summertime and my husband and I had just driven across country from Texas to Massachusetts, our hometown. We had just ETS'd (Expiration of Term of Service) out of the military and were about to begin our new life with our new son, as civilians. On the way to Massachusetts, we laughed and had a great time. My mother had flown into Texas a few days prior to pick up our first born son so that we could drive back home with some of our belongings in the back seat. It was our first time alone since the baby had been born. We rekindled so much fire during that road trip.

My husband had set up an interview in Manassas, Virginia. We were going to move there after we were officially transitioned out of the military. We drive across states and made it to the interview looking rough. We had our entire closet in the back seat of our car and smelled like junk food and "outside." I went in the interview with my husband. Looking back, it was probably inappropriate for us both the be there but it was just one of those times we didn't even think about what should have been, we just did us.

My husband got the job and we continued our drive up to Massachusetts. We were elated at the idea of a new beginning. We couldn't believe he got the job looking like a hot mess. We had to celebrate. We made up songs, told jokes and clowned around all the way home. We were unstoppable and had a working plan. Fearless, I thought. The drive from Virginia seemed to fly by. We were at my parent's house in Massachusetts before we knew it. We decided that we'd only be in Massachusetts for two weeks before transitioning to Virginia. A week and a half passed quickly. It was almost time to leave our hometown to go on the adventure of a lifetime. I remember sitting at the gas station and my husband turned to me with worry in his eyes. He was afraid. What if he failed? I had never thought of this as an option. He was afraid. In that moment he needed me to give him what he couldn't find in his own heart. He needed a little encouragement like we all do sometimes.

His fear struck me with fear. Instead of encouragement, I latched on to it, his fear. I reassured him that I had his back. With fear in my heart, I told him we could change the plan and I could find a job in Massachusetts. We were in my old stomping ground. There was some kind of job for me to hold. My knee-jerk reaction was an attempt to try to correct the fear. At that time I needed it to disappear. I need it to go away immediately. The fear I was experiencing was not a fear that kept me from believing my husband couldn't do the job or be a success at whatever he put his hand to. I knew he could. I still know he is capable. However, at that time the thing I feared the most was being weak. It was something I ran from in myself for years because of the trauma I had experienced as a child. In his question of affirmation, my husband was inviting me to a place of intimacy. I had never been there before. Therefore I was unable to embrace my husband's plea for intimacy.I wasn't ready to confront my own weakness in this intimate place. My background of being molested left me with grave intimacy issues. Hearing the words of, "what if …," felt like I was looking in a mirror. I was afraid of my husband showing a human weakness because it just wasn't something I was ready to face in myself at the time. My choice to join in the fear instead of affirming my husband was something that devastated our relationship for years after the fact. Bound by resentment on both sides, we moved on and never went to Manassas, Virginia.

Many wives have no idea how their presence can upgrade, or downgrade, their husband's life as well as the entire relationship. As a result they settle for limited capacities of mundane housework or dreams that don't make it out of the journal they wrote them in. Stifled and suffocated gifts become misplaced objects in a room full of untapped potential at a 9-5 job they hate. Sometimes women even get discouraged because of the barriers that keep them from doing, earning, or achieving the same things a man can. Nonetheless, your purpose by design is meant to be opposite of everything your husband is. This is not permission to not get along. It means your accessibility as a wife is heightened when your weaknesses are exposed and compliment each other.

In the Bible, God never designed Eve to be exactly like Adam. She was actually designed to be his mirror opposite. Eve possessed every quality, responsibility, and attribute Adam lacked. God even made Adam and Eve's sexual organs a mirror opposite so they both could enjoy the most pleasurable physical experience known to human beings. Eve was her husband's equal, endowed with an essential power that fit together perfectly for them to create life.

The traditional teaching of the woman as help (meet) is likened to that of an assistant role or someone who is subservient to the one being helped. This definition might appear to line up with a dictionary's definition of the word. However, a scripture can never mean what it has never meant. Therefore, if you look at the context of every other use of the word help or "ezer" in the Hebrew, in the scripture, you will find that ezer refers to either God or military allies. In such cases, the one giving the help is superior to the one receiving the help. Perhaps this is where some belief systems get their wires crossed. Adding kenegdo, meaning meet in the Hebrew, modifies the meaning to be that of equal rather than superior status. Other translations provide additional renditions including; "a helper fit for him" (RSV), "a helper as his partner" (NRS), "a helper comparable to him" (NKJ), "a helper as his counterpart" (YLT), and "a helper suitable for him," (NASB).

"Then the LORD God said, "It is not good for the man to be alone; I will make him a helper suitable for him."

Genesis 2:18

In the bible, Eve was created to be a helper for Adam, a helper who was suitable for him. She was created and entered the scene at his level. They were compatible; complimentary in being opposite, in vision and purpose. Our modern society has learned to shun humility ultimately missing the true interpretation of God's intention for your role as wife. It's no wonder people don't want to be married or stay married. No one knows their role. They confuse help as being a powerless doormat!

True power in a marital relationship comes when men and women understand that they have been blessed with different gifts, abilities, and responsibilities that truly work together in equal partnership to help each other be successful. Men and women need each other and it is only when they are united in body, mind, and soul, that God's work can effectively move forward.

When I matured enough to see the errors of my ways as a wife, it wasn't until deeper into our marriage. I didn't intend to discourage my husband's ideas. I was flowing too far and too deep into the rivers of fear. I was afraid to face the demons in my own past. I let them cover my faults with the duty of responsibility. By nature, I'm responsible where he's not and he is a dreamer, true visionary where I can't see. This is how we complement each other. Had I known then, what I know now, we would have been much further along in the success part of our relationship.

Knowing your power and position to upgrade your husband's life doesn't take anything away from his power. Matter of fact it enhances your power as one. Without a vision, there is nothing for you as a wife to help with. Without the help, there is no part of the vision for him to fulfill. Don't be so quick to say you don't need a man because you do, you need each other in order to fulfill the upgrade experience and not sabotage the opportunity to win in your marriage.

Chapter 3

Insane Faith

"I can't believe we're here again!"

From the time Adam and Eve entered the scene as one, God's will for marriage became no mystery. As a married couple, your mission is to build. Whether you are building a family by having lots of children or are building a business that makes lots of money, building in the form of multiplication is the way married couples get to feel God's smile on their relationship. Life circumstances sometimes make it easy to lose sight of the overall mission marriage is to accomplish. When situations happen whether it is caused by you or him, opposite of God's will, and you know it, you're supposed to feel out of place, off balance, and incomplete. When you step outside of God's covering, his path, his plan, and his way, it will be as obvious as a pimple on a baby's face. It will be uncomfortable for you and your husband in all aspects. It will cause strain in communication both verbally and physically. However, prayer will get you back on track.

My husband and I have fallen off track financially, spiritually, and emotionally many times over. From homelessness to homeownership we've been through it all. However what I've learned is the key to every set back was to be sure our bounce back was really a comeback and not a reverse. Together we had to learn to be intentional about our resilience. The ability to bounce back is your comeback to get on track, every time. As a wife, prayer is the tool you can use to identify the steps of your comeback.

Adversity will strike your marriage. It is a part of the process of achieving growth building strength as a couple. Adversity in any relationship exposes vulnerability, areas of growth. As a wife, you work hard to do your part to keep up your looks, cook, clean, be sexually desirable, while still aiming to accomplish personal goals as well. However, through all of these things, sometimes it is difficult to admit to weakness. Especially when your effort of giving your best seems to not be good enough or not produce the intended results you were seeking. Admission of weakness through adversity compels the soul to look beyond itself and cling to the grace God offers through His strength.

The opposite of adversity is to obtain well being. Being well in the marital relationship is a challenge to any weakness. When you're not ready to admit it, even then, God knows every one of your weak areas and is present to help you win over them all. Overcoming weakness can feel impossible. Especially when you think you have to do it by yourself. God promises that in your weakness His strength is made perfect. Which means you're never dealing with weakness alone. You have God's strength to lean on.

> "And He said to me, "My grace is sufficient for you, for My strength is made perfect in weakness." Therefore most gladly I will rather boast in my infirmities, that the power of Christ may rest upon me. Therefore I take pleasure in infirmities, in reproaches, in needs, in persecutions,

in distresses, for Christ's sake. For
when I am weak, then I am strong."

2 Corinthians 12: 9-10

In this scripture, the apostle Paul is talking about the efforts God took to keep him humble. He was a man who God entrusted great visions and revelations to. Even still, he had what some believe to be great trouble or perhaps even a great temptation, also known as a thorn in his flesh, that served as a point of weakness. God still brought good through Apostle Paul's weakness in the same way he does for us today. God brings us out of weak places in a way that keeps us open, vulnerable and pliable before Him and sometimes before our husbands. Prayer is a remedy for the soreness of every weak space. Sometimes weakness exposed through trouble in the marriage is sent to teach you to pray and continue the relationship with insane faith, through prayer. Though God accepts a prayer of faith, he may not always grant you what you're asking for. He sometimes grants in wrath and denies in love. Pressure and failure in a relationship can leave you as a wife feeling dizzy from a circle of defeat, too weak to admit weakness and too prideful to begin the work in becoming a stronger person through prayer. When God does not take away our troubles or temptations in the marital relationship, this scripture is a reminder of God's promise to give us enough grace to get through the presenting obstacle that is trying to delay, deny or disprove success in your marriage. Grace is enough to strengthen and comfort any weakness exposed in marital distresses. When you feel that you are too weak to face the challenges your marriage is experiencing, reach out to receive strength through an intimate place of prayer with God.

Too often weakness is criticized as laziness

or mediocrity. With this definition in mind married couples tend to dismiss the idea of weakness ever being present in their relationship. Which subsequently dismisses the presence of God's strength ever being experienced in the marriage. Too often in this place, wives and husbands alike try their best to cover up or give unnecessary validation for masking weakness, God's opportunity to make you both stronger people. Others mistake it for a lack of perfection and become overachievers in efforts to overcompensate feelings of inadequacy. Inadequacy presents an obligation to deepen the wedge between distance and intimacy in the marriage relationship. As your husband's wife, there are things that God wants to share with you, and only you, about him and about you. Secrets you as his wife, are entitled to know. Secrets He expects you to use to enhance the bond between the two of you. Secrets that he can only share behind the veil; an intimate place of prayer. Whether you've prayed one time or fifty times about a certain element of your relationship, through the lens of weakness, prayer can seem impossible to believe in.

Believing God for the same thing over and over and over again sounds crazy until God moves on His promise. Until God's promise is a manifested reality in your relationship, your girlfriends or family are going to call you crazy. But the vision you see of your husband and the change God promised to bring to the situation you're in, doesn't turn you loose. When the change is something you know God said, you can't remove the hope it is tied to from your mind or your heart. You actually have to believe in it. You need to believe and can stop believing that God will do what he said he would do. Despite what family, friends, or even what you might think in low times you must still believe your relationship will win. The insanity of your faith is what will build strength in you as a wife as well as build strength in your relationship with your husband.

When you stop believing God for the miraculous change He promised you'd have in your relationship, it's usually because you've started to become intimate with someone else. When you find yourself drifting from insane faith, it is a clear indication that you've shared too much with others about what is going on in your marriage. Your marriage is private. It is special and so is the protection of its intimacy. It is good for you both to seek wise counsel when needed. However, women tend to reach out to what is familiar and not necessarily wise counsel the relationship mutually agrees upon. In this case, when you open the bedroom door of intimacy in your relationship with others, you give access to outside influence to poison the expectation of promise. Those external forces in most cases can only deliver the opinion of self. The whispers of Satan himself into these deep places also give him access to desecrate well being and contaminate the hope you once had for your relationship. Through penetration, it blackens the core of what God put together and no man is to put asunder. As a wife, you have no time for intimacy with anyone else besides your husband. Just like with Eve, Lucifer's lies present a request for access, of which you can deny, to disturb the peace resting in the intimate quarters of your marital relationship. Upon entry, he brings nothing but chaos.

As a wife, you cannot be intimate with Satan. He will ejaculate anxiety all over your spirit. Being intimate with Satan will cause you to birth children of anxiety in your marriage. As the children of anxiety grow in your mind, they produce doubt

Wife Pray Win

and steal joy. With doubt, the desire you once had to believe in God and believe in prayer dies. Without a communicative connection to the source of life through prayer, nothing in your life or your marriage can thrive. For this reason, Satan tries hard to steal access to the most intimate places of your relationship. His ultimate goal is to disconnect you and your relationship from the source, with doubt.

Overwhelming doubt in your mind sounds like, "he will never change," "things will never be different," "things will never be the same," "I'm stuck," "we're hopeless," "I need a new man," and so on. Spreading like a wild fire, doubt will turn around and re-impregnate you with anger. Whether big or small, you will find yourself getting angry with it all. Satan wants your anger to grow into full-blown rage because rage obstructs the view of purpose. Consequently, when the anger

54

subsides or is resolved what's left is what is true. What is true is that behind the anger, Satan knows you love your husband and have purpose to build together. Despite the efforts of the adversary, prayer will help you restrict access to what doesn't belong to anyone but God.

Satan can only use what you give him access to see. When he is allowed to see what goes on in the bedroom chambers of your marriage he knows what vices can be manipulated to cause division where there is supposed to be harmony, growth, and love. He will do everything in his power to distract you both from connecting, being able to find common ground. That's why it only takes one minute for you to go from being mad as hell with your husband to being madly in love or missing him like crazy. You're not crazy when this happens. You're being played like a fiddle by the Pied Piper. When you see yourself demonstrating these mixed messaged behaviors, know that they serve as notification to the fact that somewhere along the way you gave external forces access to the sacred spaces of your marriage; access that must be revoked immediately.

Satan wants your relationship to die. It is only through prayer that God can resurrect any dead place in your relationship. If you ask him, He will guide you on how to get Satan's whispers, seeds, and chaos out of the intimate places of your marriage. He will lead you by exposing your weaknesses. Confess them. Confess to God what's behind your anger. It might hurt. Tell God anyway. Tell him what you're so mad about. Tell God how disappointed you feel. He wants to hear it. He wants you to unload all of your weaknesses because He cares about you. Through the exposition of your weakness, He wants to show you what turning your weakness into His strength looks like in your relationship. Your confession to God breaks the chains of bondage Satan has in your marriage. Confession of weakness is the beginning of Satan's exit from your intimate marital quarters and the beginning of your decision to believe in your marriage, again.

The scripture says that out of the mouth flows the rivers of the heart (Luke 6:45). As it relates to prayer, when we decide to pray we are communicating to God from the truth that rests in our heart. This means that when you have negative emotions and negative memories in your heart they can be a block to the flow of your prayers. If then they are a block to your prayers, they can keep your mind from believing in your relationship success. They can even keep your mind from believing prayer will work. As a wife, you can let nothing get in between the flow of your prayers to God for your marriage. You can let no negative emotion go avoided. Negative emotions are not bad and are not to be ignored. They are to be addressed. Your prayers are most effective when they come from a pure heart. Not a perfect heart, but a heart that knows it needs God. Without a clean heart, your lack of belief won't let your prayers reach the throne of grace. Things like holding resentment toward your husband for whatever he didn't do or for whatever he did do, will not enhance your prayers. Further, emotional blockage disregards the power God holds to change the situation. Trying to hold on to things only God can handle is not your role as your husbands a wife. You can't change your husband's but you can always pray for him and pray for peace in your marriage.

Peace in your marriage comes from confidence in God. Nothing will be perfect. In the same way, pain from exposing weakness won't last always. Though a righteous man falls seven times, he will get up (Proverbs 24:16). Be resilient. If your relationship has taken a fall financially, spiritually, physically, or emotionally, with insane faith, get back on track one more time.

A Call To Pray

Father, forgive me.

I ask you to help me forgive myself so that I
can embrace your call to be my husband's wife.

I invite you into my heart to show me what

you want me to be focused on,

what you want to be different,

and how you want me to be a better

wife in my marriage.

Amen

PRAY

"Call to me and I will answer you,

and will tell you great and hidden things that

you have not known."

Jeremiah 33:3

Chapter 4

Team Correct-A-Seed

"You're doing this for the vine."

Your assignment to your husband is bigger than the image of what and who you are together. It is even bigger than anything you can materialistically accomplish as one. God's intention for your marital relationship is aligned with the fruitfulness of what can be produced from your union. The enemy is after just that; the fruit of your union. If he can get you to stop producing fruit from your relationship, he can shut down your legacy from establishing generational blessing or even cause your legacy's existence to be dormant. The fight is never after the simplicity of dividing you and your husband's relationship. The fight against your marriage is for the conquering of your entire lineage. Satan and his cohorts will use any little or big distraction as a vice to conquer. Satan wants the seed, the fruit, the favor of every single thing that flows from you, as one. He wants to kill, steal, and destroy the legacy of blessing that God ordained to flow through what the two of you are able to produce together. As the growth in your marriage focuses more on creating, defining, and enhancing legacy, your role as a wife is grounded in protecting that legacy and being spiritually conscious enough to fortify it.

Multigenerational Stresses & Oppression
Stress ignites pressure. Pressure forces behavior.

The choice of behavior displayed in any given situation challenges what you know to be right and what you've seen to be true. If when growing up you saw momma always yelling at her man, married or not. Your first opportunity without even thinking about it is going to express your anguish in the same chaotic communication. Behavioral responses to stressors in your marriage are determined not only by the environment, and your present interactions but also by the environment you grew up in with (or without) your parents. In recent studies, evidence has been found that suggests responses to environmental conditions can also persist over multiple offspring generations, having a transgenerational effect (Groot, M.P., Kooke, R., Knoben, N., Vergeet, P., Keurentjes, J. J. B., Ouborg, N.J., & Verhoeven, K.J.F., 2016). Whatever your choice of behavior in response to stressors, develops the environment of the seed your marriage produces and grows out of.

Remember when your husband didn't pick up his clothes off of the floor? He just stepped out of them, left them on the floor and kept on about his business. Remember that? You were probably fuming with anger. In that anger, how did you react? Did you respond like you've always seen all the women in your family respond? Did you even notice you were repeating what you saw or didn't see growing up? When you reflect on what type of behaviors you choose in conflict or any level of communication, think about where it is coming from and who is watching. Whether you realize it or not your children, (or those in your circle of influence), are watching, paying very close attention, better than they do in school, to how you respond in relationships. If what you've shown them so far is contrary to what you now know to be a better choice, take time to meet with them, reset, and "correct-a-seed." Otherwise the same triggers of generational stress that you or your husband struggle with will counter-produce the blessings your legacy is meant to experience.

Stress results in persistent and intersecting impacts on the mindset of women, to include their spiritual and mental health (McGibbon & McPherson, 2013). Stress can seduce the mind to believe oppressing opinions that prevent you from exercising your spiritual authority, through prayer, as a wife. From stress, an oppressed mindset can avert progression in the growth and building of your marriage and have a long-lasting impact on your perception of your marriage or of your husband. Meaning, the impact of stress on the way that you think, can convince your mind to believe that the relationship is not going to work or it is not worth the work required to make it work. This level of stress, with the outlook of failure, is a form of a repressive and destructive distraction to your marriage.

Stress explodes at the point of intersect between three main relational areas. They are social - the outside influences allowed in your marriage, identity conflicts - finding purpose in self-existence outside of the relationship, and geography - the environment the relationship is being cultivated in. At the point any one of these areas cross, stress is eminent. Stress comes from being torn between the present state and the goal state. Stress is a form of conflict, in this case, internal and spiritual (conflict). It is the battle you face when something happens unexpectedly or doesn't turn out the way you hoped or envisioned. How you choose to handle these stresses connected to your marriage can invite growth or empower wreckage in your relationship.

This means that if you're going through a broke phase, it's going to be a trigger for stress. If you're unable to find your purpose outside of your wifely duties, that's going to end up being a trigger for stress. And if you're living in a location, area, or environment that is toxic for your marriage to develop healthy tendencies, that is also going to be a trigger for stress as an oppression. When arisen, these conflicts signal an urgency for you to re-examine how you think about your marriage. Give direct attention to the stresses that arise to avoid giving weight to the oppression and its perpetuation of developing an oppressive legacy; verbally and nonverbally, within your marriage. Otherwise, you will find yourself unable to sustain the mental struggle between hope, change, and growth. A reality that will be felt most by those watching your relationship unfold.

Multigenerational Connections & Blessings

My parents are a tremendous example of a curse-breaking love. They were trailblazers who to this day, demonstrate that generational success can be established. Their offspring are then the demonstration of generational success replicated. My husband and I had to find our own way to pass along and enhance what generational success should look like. That is the responsibility of replicating blessings; repeat and increase or enhance, make better.

I remember when we were new in our marriage, year four or five to be exact. We served in the military and moved all over the country as gypsies trying to find our way. For the most part, we were friendly and open to meeting all types of new people. However, it didn't take long for me to realize even mosquitos are attracted to light. Unfortunately, I didn't always know what to do about it. Like a mosquito, it was an annoying distraction to have the wrong people so deeply connected to the cherished spaces of our marital relationship. Let's just say I lost my cool at a few cookouts. It was a struggle and the struggle was real. Finally, after a few crazy nights, tears, and yelling, I reached out to my mentor who instructed me to pray. She always told me to pray, often times after spiritually scolding me. I'm convinced, spiritual spankings hurt more than physical ones. Nonetheless, in obedience, and not always willingly, I heeded the instruction. Over time, I noticed the more I prayed, the more people started to drop away. Looking back, I recognize and thank God for their falling away. It had to happen in order for us as a couple to shift to our next level. Everyone is not coming with you in the shift.

Understand that the people in your network, their ideas, and their mindset about money and relationship must align to or aid in the progression of your marriage. Otherwise, no matter how nice a person is, there is nothing in common. Without anything in common, there is only distraction.

The enemy holds no punches. He'll use whatever distraction he sees gets under your skin. The only way to thwart his plans is to take authority in prayer. As a wife, your prayers must cover you, him, and the seed; everything that flows from the two of you to include children, dreams, visions, and power, the ultimate legacy of generational blessings. Even before it is manifested, prayer is your weapon of protection. Protecting your union's purpose through prayer happens when the sins in the bloodline are released. The sins of thought and behaviors and decisions that misalign to God's intended will for your relationship must be detached from your legacy. When you pray know that, "these signs shall follow them that

believe; In my name shall they cast out devils..."
(Mark 16:17). You are empowered to change the
trajectory of your legacy through seed prayers that
correct what entered in your legacy through a sin
that repeatedly became a curse.

Chapter 5

Real Talk. Real Prayer.

"But, I do pray for my husband…"

Do you really pray for your husband? Praying for God to move in or through your husband for your benefit, is not praying for him. Sure things are tough right now. Sure you're tired of seeing him down, depressed, or rejected from life. Sure you want change and are sick of how things are. But a selfish prayer will never produce lasting results. Selfishness belongs on the alter, not smeared over the forehead of your husband. Check yourself. As a wife, when you seek to manipulate your husband in prayer for selfish gain, it is often based on pride. Humility is the solution.

Most women can easily come up with ways their men fail to demonstrate love yet miss the plank hanging out of their own eye. There were so many times I prayed prayers about all of the things I felt my husband was doing wrong. In return, I'd hear from God a laundry list of things I needed to work on. At the time, I felt like, "But God, did you hear all of the other things I said? Don't you see what he's doing?" I didn't feel like my prayers were being addressed because God's response pointed back to me making more changes within myself. I didn't connect the need for my change to the end result of making the relationship better. I didn't realize the power of influence I had from being on my knees. The reality was that there was work for God to do in me. God was trying to draw me closer to him through prayer. There were things He needed to teach me about myself, about my life and about my husband. Things I could only get from him. Things that would positively influence my marriage.

Your influence as a wife is a power that is the most potent when used to give glory to God and not to edify selfish gain. When you feel anxious about your influence or are tempted by manipulation, go to God with your unmet needs and disappointments. Go to God with your frustration of being misunderstood. Prayer is what pries the manipulating fingers of influence off the heart and soul of your husband. It sets you both free to grow closer to one another. It breaks down the wall of pride so that humility can saturate your relationship.

Some of the circumstances that cripple a relationship come from pride. Pride emerges from abuse, betrayal, and overall disrespect. Pride is a layer of protection some people use to cover a personal vulnerability. Often times it may seem easier to hide behind pride than to be exposed to the truth of what needs to be changed within. Consider your last confrontation with your husband. If you lied and said everything was ok during the confrontation when it was not, you have deceived your husband and disrespected your relationship. Deceiving your husband through dishonest communication only sabotages your relationship with him. If you pretend with him, mask your feelings with pride by being guarded or misleading, you deny him the chance to really get to know you. You also refuse the opportunity to really get to know him. Before you know it, you'll be living with a stranger. Then the communication between the two of you becomes a method of communication in your relationship tool kit that you only use to get what you want. As complete dishonor to him as an equal, your relationship is robbed of its value further isolating your husband by putting a wall between the two of you.

Plain and simple, deception and manipulation are emotional instruments used to avoid confrontation. For this reason, deception and manipulation kill marriages because they are the opposite of respect and honor. Instead of using tactics of deception, value your husband's feelings and give them respect, even if they are uncomfortable to hear at first. I remember the first time my husband told me how he really felt in confrontation. It shocked me for two reasons; I didn't like that it highlighted my weaknesses and I didn't like that he was right. Subsequent to the discomfort, hearing him trust me with holding his heart by sharing his perspective about me or whatever was going on in our relationship at that time, helped me to look at praying for him in a different way. It helped me to see the value he held for our relationship. It affirmed why God put us together and demonstrated that together we can enjoy a real and meaningful relationship built on trust; sharing the truth about everything.

As a wife, being afraid to lose an argument defeats the mission to win the war. This means you can and will be wrong sometimes. Allowing yourself to be wrong is a position of humility. Humility is the tool God uses to draw you closer to one another and closer to Him. Losing an argument, if that is how you choose to interpret it, is not a loss of power. It is a redirection of power that God wants you to utilize in its rightful capacity; prayer. Women who don't know any better use this power to entice men and open the door for rebellion in the relationship. Wives use this power to protect, please and build up their husbands. Only honesty and openness through prayer build a deepened marital relationship.

Manipulation creates big messes. Women in the bible who manipulated their way go as far back as the beginning. Eve (Genesis 1-3) was created as equal to Adam, in God's image. Both had the same responsibility of obedience to their Creator. Yet she held a profound power to influence that was bent to replace God's will with her own. She used her influence to wound her relationship. There was also, Sarah. Sarah (Genesis 11-23) had a difficult time following Abrams's call by God. Her flaw was in running ahead of God's promise to give offspring in the matter of Hagar (Genesis 16). Her anxiety led her to jealousy, vengeance, and shifting blame (16:5). She influenced her husband to act against the promises of God by having a child, named Ishmael, outside of God's promise. And finally, there was Rebekah (Genesis 24-26). She was an intelligent, strong-willed woman. What God promised her, she forced to bring it about. Her manipulation of Jacob (Genesis 27) ultimately backfired. Her influence got her, her own way through deception in showing favoritism towards "the son she loved."

Like these women, there is no level of perfection you will ever reach. Each one of these women were convinced there was a better way. They were persuaded to believe that the better way would have to come through them. However, their flaw was in allowing their lack of faith, trust, and humility blind the better way God already promised. But here's the kicker. One of the greatest things about God is that there is always a way, a possibility and opportunity to present your heart as pure when you pray. It happens through humility. The humility in admitting to selfish prayer, intentions, thoughts, and language releases power to say prayers that move heaven and earth in a way that revolutionizes the bond of your marital relationship.

Misusing prayer and misusing your power as a wife to pray, is synonymous with working witchcraft. Even so, the secret to winning in marriage is to hope in God and not give way to fear, pride, or selfishness. As you put hope in God (not your husband), focus your efforts on being the woman God created you to be. Pray expectantly without fear. You just might be given a front row seat to see God do abundantly more than you could ever ask or imagine in your marriage.

Chapter 6

Boundaries & Distractions

"I can't pray for him. I don't know what to say."

When your relationship is getting ready to experience growth, it will simultaneously experience challenge. The only way to strengthen your relationship is by challenging its current strength. The only way to challenge the strength of your relationship for purposes of growth is to expose the weak areas of your individual character, relational boundaries, and individual motive.

Challenge for change in a marital relationship comes in various forms of exposure to each one of these areas of growth.

Individual Character

Your individual psychology heavily contributes to the health of your marriage. Immaturity in character will bruise the healing confrontation is intended to bring. In a marriage, you're going to disagree on things that may lead to an argument and that is ok. Women are deceived by the idea that it is better to change their husband than deal with the tsunami of emotional baggage typically brought into the relationship by holding back. This belief system couldn't be farther from the truth. In a dysfunctional relationship, you can end up spending so much time working through baggage that you never get to begin working on the building part. Sometimes it feels like there is just too much to unpack. But you have to unpack before you can build.

Individual character defects can lie at the root of your marital problems. Denying character defects can leave you in a place of blaming each other for problems in the marriage (Jacobs, 2009). Besides being unfair it makes it harder to address and fix issues that arise. If you really want to experience a change in your relationship it will be important to make the choice to work on your personal flaws. Doing so will dramatically change the functionality of your marriage.

Relational Boundaries

The person or people you go to for help in your marriage should be a person or people who you and your husband agree to trust to pour into your relationship. The idea of sharing all of your hearts hurts with your girlfriends while you're going through a tough time is nice, but not realistic. Most often, not impactful or beneficial. Your relationship is a three strand cord (Ecclesiastes 4:12). There is no tighter bond that can be formed. The strands represent you, your husband, and God. While there may be people around you that love you both, their love for you or your relationship cannot be the only qualifying factor that gives them permission to speak, have an opinion or give advice in your relationship. Who you and your husband choose as a marriage mentor can serve as a guardian for the next dimension of your relationship. Mentoring is a common way to pass on knowledge or skills. The relationship mentor holds the neutral space of accountability for you both. They are not a parent, therapist, or friend. In the capacity of mentor, they are usually in your life for a term or a season, to help guide your relationship to get or stay on track. The relationship is unique and dynamic in support of keeping the standard of marital success in tact.

The standard of marital success is enforced through boundaries and unrelenting non-negotiables. Everything in creation has boundaries. The sea and the sand have boundaries. The sea does not go but so far onto shore before it draws back to itself. It respects the order of water and land, an order established by God. Therefore boundaries represent a reverence for order. In the same way, integrity is an essential boundary to the standard of marital success. When things get crazy, a person with integrity owns up to their portion of responsibility and is willing to work toward a solution. An integrous woman, a wife, is not afraid of her flaws. She respects them. She embraces them because they represent an opportunity for growth, change, and greener grass on the other side of her marital problems. The respect for order keeps her from blowing up and tearing down everything in her path.

Faith is another essential boundary to the standard of marital success. The scripture says, "Do not be yoked together with unbelievers," (2 Corinthians 6:14). To be honest, I've questioned this scripture at least once or twice. I struggled with what it really meant to be "equally yoked" in a relationship. There can be many different dynamics, complications, and complexities at various stages of growth in a marriage. For this reason, I wondered the meaning of equally yoked and if by definition, wondered could it be one that blanketed every situation. I wanted God to be pleased with my life, my marriage, and my choices, but there were moments where I doubted if my husband and I were meant to be. Things didn't "look" like they were "supposed" to all the time. Matter of fact, there were times we both questioned our union. Our relationship seemed so different from the church people we were around.

Yet so perfect for the two of us. It was only through prayer and really getting to know my husband's heart and really letting him hold mine, that I learned how different, special, and God-ordained our relationship really was.

Establishing a boundary of faith is not as simple as finding out whether or not someone is a Christian. It's not about their role in the church or how many church services they attend. It's about how their faith is expressed in their life. It's about you praying and asking God to reveal the truth or reason why He brought the two of you together. There is promise, truth, and wisdom to be gleaned in this level of prayer. If you are in a position that questions your yoke, get in God's presence so He can give you affirmed resolve about your union. Beyond the eyes of everyone watching, judging, or talking only God knows what He's really put together. He knows the parts of your heart you haven't shown each other yet. Only He knows how much you and your husband need each other. Only He has your answer.

Commitment is also a pillar in the boundaries of the standard for marital success. Genuine commitment to make your relationship work honors God and honors each other. Commitment is about seeing the end goal of wellness no matter the trial. Goals are the way to keep your marriage on track and moving forward. Without goals, your relationship might stagnate and even regress. When setting your relationship goals, a detailed plan is not necessary, necessarily. However, if you have few goals for the future, living in the moment is fun only for a short while. When that moment is over, your relationship may be left in a place of chaos mixed with reluctant confusion to move forward, together. An outcome contradictory to the pillar of commitment.

When boundaries have been crossed and lines are blurred, you are supposed to feel upset. You're supposed to want to confront things. You're supposed to identify with the flag that your spirit is waving against the standard that is not being met or is being violated. Violations are not to be ignored, given permission, or given an excuse for. Take the boundary offense to God in prayer. He will show you how to recalibrate your love for your husband and yourself or help you to initiate the re-exploration of your marriage's non-negotiables.

Non-negotiables are simply the needs you have and can't compromise. Every person in every relationship comes with a set of needs. Classifying your needs as non-negotiable are what separates them from being mere "wants." If you want to be in a growing kind of relationship with your husband, you will choose to meet his needs. You will also commit to your relational needs being met by him alone. An inability or unwillingness to meet the needs of your husband is one reason why many relationships experience conflict and sometimes dissolve. Needs are non-negotiable. Nevertheless, the way they get met is at the place where you both compromise.

You may not always understand why your husband needs something, and you don't have to (always understand). Sometimes you won't have the words to explain to him why you have an eminent need as well. In both cases, respect it. Likewise, as a wife, be careful not to meet the needs of your husband and ignore or undermine your needs. Often times wives will do anything just to keep their husband happy or even keep him around. When done at the expense of neglecting personal needs, you'll be surprised by feelings of unhappiness or discontent roaring like a lion until you can't function. Relationships work, thrive, and prosper when people are willing to respect one another's needs and work together to find a solution that makes you both happy and the relationship stable.

Individual Motive

When is the last time you forgave your husband? Are you still holding onto something he did or didn't do? Did you think it was too small (or too big) to bring up? Why? These are the questions every wife has to ask herself when measuring her motive. The measure of your motive can impact or alter how you respond to challenges, changes, discussion, or conflict. In the heat of an argument, you may think its time to call it quits. When things get tough, you may both find yourselves saying things like, "I'm done." However, if you're honest, your motive in wanting to move on, away from your husband, may be driven by hurt from a violation of boundaries gone unaddressed.

Therefore instead of trying to get away from your husband, the truth driving your motive is really a strong attempt to get away from the problem. A constant evaluation of your motive, sometimes in the moment, will help you separate the difference.

Problems are often very hard to confront. Especially when they point out your flaws to which your husband, the one who knows all and has front row seat to every scene of your life, is pointing out. Regardless of the position or perception or out of any argument, trial, or disastrous situation your marriage needs to be able to get over, through, and keep moving beyond the (present) pain. If your motive is not pure to believe moving forward is possible, or if it is distracted by hurt, blocked by negative emotions or the outside voices in your relationship, it is time to check your motive. As a wife, let your motive keep you honest to the hurts in your heart so that they do not manifest as impure and increased strife in your relationship.

When there is a violation within any one of these areas of relational growth it will reveal the vulnerabilities within your relationship that are exposed to the risk of growth stagnation. Or, whose pain is preventing you from doing so. Setting boundaries, measuring motives, and warding off emotional distraction help to minimize the dissolution of what God, assuming you didn't pick your own man, intended to be a journey of unprecedented growth; building between you and your husband. It also helps you work through the heart of unforgiveness.

Unforgiveness is an intentional, harmful process by which a victim is consumed by the holding on of negative emotion toward an offense. With that negative emotion, negative energy flows within every part of the person; mind, body, and spirit. Further, at every chance it gets, it skews the perception of and chokes the opportunity in being able to experience any positive influence a healthy marriage, has to offer.

Unforgiveness doesn't always identify itself with a red suit and a pitchfork. Naturally, if we were able to see the toxicity that festers on the inside, on the outside, it'd be easy to pin-point, heal from, and remove from our lives. It can be hard to find within, and when found, make you feel like you were tricked. The goal of the enemy is to trick you. If he can trick you, he can destroy your relationship. The goal in tricking you is an attempt to get you to believe you're over something that is still eating you up like cancer. If you believe you forgave a certain offense but have not forgiven the offense holistically, then instead of experiencing the joy of a healed and healthy relationship, you're only experiencing healing in part. Being healed only in part means a piece of you is broken which also means you're loving, your husband, only in part. If a piece of you is broken, not getting the attention it needs to heal, and only loving in part, eventually, that piece of you will die. If there is a piece of you that dies from brokenness, there will be a gap in your marriage only God can repair.

Coloring this concept in real life, imagine that you and your husband agree he is going to be responsible for taking out the trash. You notice that he takes out the trash, but not from around the entire house. You mention it to him and he still proceeds to only take out the trash that is in one particular location. You're sick of him avoiding your request and speak to him about it. His response communicates that you should be thankful he is even doing the trash because he works all day. You decided not to argue and leave it alone. Naturally, as time passes, you start to feel some type of way.

The issue or remnant of the issue re-presents itself every time you notice trash in another room. Until there is resolve, to include compromise, you may find your frustration turns into misery, turning then into disrespect, into resentment, into anger, turned negative in every aspect of expression your marriage can have.

When you have a big heart, its easy to get hurt and over time, very hard to forgive. I remember thinking I had forgiven people in general only to discover the pain therein seeping into my marriage. I wanted to forgive because I wanted to be free from the hurt I felt. One relational trauma after the next only taught me how to better dismiss the hurt all together. Dismissing an issue and forgiving an issue are two completely different things. Time after time, person after person, I dismissed hurt that I didn't realize wasn't forgiven. To survive in my marriage, I found a way to separate the offense from the forgiveness of the act from, as well as from the forgiveness of the emotion it inflicted. Because I had dismissed the issue, I subsequently detached the emotional pain from the experience. Later the sting of hurt resurrected through triggers of similar actions and came back with a vengeance in my marriage. I just couldn't shake it off. What I learned later was that God didn't want me to shake it off. He wanted me to address the root and stop plucking the leaves on the tree of hurt that grew in my heart. At the dawn of a new day, God called me to reconcile my heart with him so that I can present my self as pure (not perfect), humble, and able to be used by him in my marriage and beyond. With hurt and pain laying dormant in your heart, you won't be able to manifest miracles, blessings, signs, and wonders in all of God's wondrous power. It will only flow in part. To win in your marriage it is time for you to begin a commitment to healing the residue of your heart's hurt before it hardens.

As a wife, the importance of maintaining a pliable heart toward your husband can be found in the scripture. Throughout scripture Christ teaches that we must look first to God's original intent for marriage; to commit to a lifelong bond between one man and one woman (Matthew 19:4–6; Genesis 2:24). Life decisions can sometimes get in the way of remembering God's original purpose. Hurt can be blinding and unforgiveness can produce a hardness of heart. In the same way, a hardened heart can destroy covenant. Moses, a prophet, and leader in the scriptures presented a bill of divorce (to the people) because of the hardness of their (the married couples) hearts (Mark 10:4). Had unforgiveness not been able to take root deep into the hearts of wives (and husbands alike), there would be no broken relationships, and hence, no divorce. To avoid a hardness of heart, we must submit to God's authority by communicating with God on the heart level.

The danger in carrying unforgiveness decays relationships the most when too much time has passed. Over time, unforgiveness can look more and more like normal life; you can miss it that easily because as women we're so good at masking the pain with many other things. However it's sting can become a permanent staple in your relationship, to the point where you don't even feel it anymore. It's numbing. It's complicated and tries to mask itself in the wild flow of resentment. The psychology of resentment is built from repetitious anguish. It's more than something you never got over. Resentment is embedded in inequality. If you feel that your husband doesn't do enough or hasn't done enough over the years, if you don't already, it won't be long before resentment can creep in and harden your heart.

Carrying resentment makes it hard to demonstrate physical affection. No matter your love language, your relationship will not survive without physical touch and regular consummation. On the contrary, in the place of resentment, you don't want to be touched. Resentment can even create feelings of not wanting to talk to or be touched by your husband at all. Yet the complexities of your feelings and the commitment you have for marriage make it difficult to let go of. Overwhelmed by the feelings of being stuck, the struggle will leave you in despair of no resolve, no hope, and no chance of returning to the place where love once felt right, warm, enjoyable, and harmonious. Even in those difficult moments, it's not over. Sometimes the struggle presents its strongest case when God is trying to get you to admit that you don't like what's going on. It is okay to disapprove of an action or circumstance. God just wants you to bring the honesty of your pain to Him. It is in these moments that change can begin. Change is preempted by conversation, first with God, then with self, and your husband.

Unforgiveness and resentment paralyze your relationship if you do not choose to address or communicate their presence with your husband. Drawing closer to God in times when it hurts, when you hurt, when you're both hurt, will help you to exercise your power to speak life to your husband, yourself, and the marriage as a whole.

As a spirit with a soul in a body, we are multidimensional beings. For this reason, forgiveness has to be explored on multiple levels. When unpacking forgiveness, it must be explored on the body, soul, and spirit level. Most people only forgive on the mind level. They decide to forgive, never confronting the emotions tied to the "forgiveness." The problem is if you have only forgiven on one of those levels you haven't yet experienced true forgiveness in your marriage. Not being able to experience true forgiveness in your marriage leave gaps in your soul, your relationship, and your body; which will only break down, become vulnerable for attack. As a wife, you must personally explore each level of forgiveness or unforgiveness to ensure that your relationship doesn't incur areas of openness for the enemy to come into and destroy. When he sees an opening, he's going to go for it every time.

Sometimes the access you give the enemy comes by way of you sharing the pain you feel in your marriage with the wrong people. Your friends are your friends for a reason. You love them and they love you. The same applies to family. However, their perspective of you and your marriage is limited to what you tell them. Their insight is limited to what they can see or assume. They are not God; all knowing, all powerful. Although they may give excellent advice, they will never know more about your marriage than God. In their love for you, there is a strong possibility that they will worry about the failure of your relationship when God is at work in your relationship. Don't let others put their worry on your faith. Keep believing God for the work He is doing in your marriage. He will finish the good work He started. Your friends and family don't know and may clearly be unable to see that your current situation is not your final destination. For that reason, they may not go with you to the next level of wins your marriage is about to experience. Keep your friends and family in perspective. Any deeper engagement will be a risk you take and a distraction you chose to entertain.

Forgiving the people, places, and things that have distracted your marital relationship requires you as a wife, to be honest with God, your husband and yourself. For the things that are tough to address or speak about, allow the holy spirit to intercede on your behalf. The Lord wants you to pray and intercede for your husband and your marriage. Keep praying that the Lord will break the chains of bondage or open your spiritual eyes to see love again or still. Then, start praising and thanking God for what He is doing. It will be distraction free and undeniable. Never give up on your husband or on God!

A Call to Pray

Father, help my husband to release

the hurt that blocks his vision.

Heal the pain of his past that is

paralyzing his future.

Help me to see the ways I can

assist his healing and not be in the way of it.

Thank you, Lord, for your grace and mercy.

Forgive me for holding onto

the darkness of hurtful things.

Forgive my unbelief and distrust for

not giving it to you sooner. Forgive me for

the lack of faith and unawareness. Help me,

work with me, and gently put the broken pieces

of my hurt heart back together again so that

I can pray and be fully used by you.

Do not let me fall victim to the controlling

words of my own negative voice.

Help me to recognize when

I'm hurting and bring it to you.

Help me to stabilize my life on your Word.

Give me the discernment and foresight to

see the enemy from afar, in whatever way

he tries to come for my marriage.

Grant me the wisdom to see

through manipulative tactics.

Dress me for battle in the spirit.

Prepare me for any mental attack that

the enemy tries to throw my way.

Saturate my soul with your love.

Abba, I trust you.

I trust that you will never leave or

forsake our family. I trust in the man of God

you have given me in my husband.

I declare that he WILL rise up

and be the man of God you ordained

for him to be, faithful, strong and committed to the call of being a man of valor, dignity, and integrity. I declare that he WILL walk as a King and use his God-given gifts to create wealth even as his soul prospers.

I declare that he will exercise decision-making that reflects your will. Constantly remind him of who he is when we're together and apart. Remind him even amongst the wolves and soul snatchers.

Keep him safe. Keep his mind, heart, and spirit at peace.

Amen

WIN

"But they that wait on the Lord

shall renew their strength;

they shall mount up with wings like eagles;

they shall run and not be weary;

they shall walk and not faint."

Isaiah 40:31

Chapter 7

This Means War

"Not in my house!"

Engaging in spiritual warfare on behalf of your relationship shifts the altitude your marriage will soar on. Spiritual warfare has a bi-present orientation. It is either offensive or defensive. Offensive spiritual warfare in a marriage happens when there is a need to tear down strongholds the enemy put in your mind, through deception, temptation, or accusations. Defensive spiritual warfare in a marriage is necessary when there is a need to guard yourself or your husband against the strategies or plans of the devil. As wives who pray, we know that the struggle is not against flesh and blood as said in Ephesians 6:12, "For we wrestle not against flesh and blood, but against principalities, against powers, against the rulers of the darkness of this world, against spiritual wickedness in high places." In this struggle against the demonic forces of deception, temptation, and accusation, you can easily be deceived by the perception that your husband is the only contributor to your current marital problem. In God's eyes, the both of you need work. You can also be tempted to cuss and curse your husband all the way out for hurting you the way he did. This struggle, is the one most women have a tough time recognizing as a trick from the enemy because of their uncontrollable emotions. You may also find yourself wanting to accuse him of past experiences. Meaning, you want to blame him when you are the one holding everything he's ever done wrong in the relationship, over his head; setting covenant bombs loose, shackling bondages of emotions to your marriage, and petting strongholds.

When there is a stronghold in your marriage, it means that a negative pattern of belief about your relationship, based on a lie, has overtaken you or your husband's mind. Strongholds are built upon lies that we have been fed. Therefore the way to tear them down is by feeding your mind the truth through the word of God. Feeding your mind the opposite of the lie Satan convinced you of is making use of the weapon spoken of in Ephesians 6:17, "...the sword of the Spirit, which is the word of God." A sword, the word of God, is an offensive weapon and is meant to tear down and kill the enemy's cohorts coming for your marital defeat. These same strongholds are the assets the devil uses against wives in the war for their marriage.

The love I have for my husband and children mean everything to me. It's an indescribable bond we share as a unit. One that I couldn't be more grateful for. But in times of the past when I felt like our bond was being threatened, I didn't pray. I got scared. I believed the stronghold, the lie, that said the love I experienced in my marriage wasn't real or wouldn't last. I believed that I wasn't really wanted by my husband, I couldn't be. I was too tainted from my childhood experiences of sexual abuse for anyone to want the real me. Let alone love the real me. Even growing up, I felt like the "dirty girl." When I got married, not much about that self-perceived feeling changed. I used to think, who wants the "dirty girl?" For years, I believed the lie that like many other social relationships I had and failed, I was only being used (in my marriage). None of which was true. God loved me purely through this time. Through my husband, God showed me how to do the work that would reveal what love really was. In breaking these strongholds through prayer, I learned that you can't pray for your husband in power without power. Fear barricades power. In fear and insecurity, you are powerless to fight for your marriage and win. There is an art to fighting for your marriage. The process therein carries power. As a wife, breaking through fear means you have to pray with mountain moving, stronghold breaking power.

Just like marriage, every great story has conflict. Learning how to fight fair in conflict, knowing what you're actually fighting and fighting for, will help to strengthen your marital relationship and give you as a wife power to fight and win. Conflict affords married couples the opportunity to better know each other. Sometimes you just can't see things in their right perspective until everything is ruffled, scattered, and out of place or in conflict. Often times people fear conflict. The reality is, it's not the conflict that is bad. It's how you handle it that makes the difference. Conflict with your husband doesn't just reveal what he's doing wrong. It also uncovers what's hiding or immature in you. Looking at the woman in the mirror is harder than pointing the finger at your husband. Even when you're right in your accusations, you are wrong for not including yourself in the equation of the problem. In marital conflict, owning it, is understanding that there is always something for both parties to learn from in every situation. God wants you to explore conflict through prayer. In this place of prayer He will reveal the ways you must heal yourself and war for your marriage.

When in conflict with your husband, prayer sometimes is not the first thing you think of. Likewise, it's not the only thing you're accountable for during and after the moment a quarrel has subsided. In conflict, consider these tips to help you heal through it. Identify what you feel. Then explore why you feel this way.

As a defense, your first inclination in conflict is to say, "Everything is fine," when you know good and well it's not. Wives and husbands alike use this position of defense as a mechanism to protect themselves from the opposite spouse being able to hurt their feelings again. If the defense could translate into words, "I'm fine," would translate into something like, "I really don't trust you to handle my feelings so I will keep them behind this wall, close to me, where they are safe." Conflict arises from lack of communication. In a marriage, when you can't communicate, you can't convert your marital problems to solutions. An inability to communicate is usually a sign that trust, even on the smallest level, is broken.

Amidst a break down of trust, communicating your feelings that are shooting off like a finale of fireworks on the fourth of July, can get lost in the pain of conflict. It will be beneficial to your relationship to evaluate your emotional temperature. When you're getting close to bursting the thermometer of emotions, take a moment to explore the genesis of the emotion displaying. If you feel something but can't put your finger on what "it" is, ask God to reveal to you the point of struggle, so you can identify the point of healing, for you and your marriage.

Focus on the Fight

With the tsunami of emotions roaring high in a moment of conflict, it can be easy to lose sight of the sound of reason, peace, compromise, and resolve. Your emotions can have you bringing up the rear of stuff you were supposed to have forgiven. Don't be deceived by their relevance. Your feelings do matter. The issues that are arising matter also. However, in a moment of conflict, self-control is more effective. Try not to be so quick in remembering all of the things your husband has ever done wrong at the moment you're supposed to be resolving one particular issue. It may pull on your level of patience to discuss one problem at a time. The deception of emotion in marital conflict is to sideswipe the progress of your communication in efforts to damage the future solution. Therefore to resolve the conflict at hand, you must communicate or compromise. The opportunities for growth are designed to birth out of compromise. Compromise can only come with clear communication and focus on the present conflict.

The Means War

Use words that help your point not harm your partner. There comes a point in every marriage when you decide divorce is not going to be an option for resolve. Making divorce a non-factor uses words that help keep you focused on expressing how you feel with language that does not demean your husband. Whether you are right or wrong, the most powerful words you can use will not be intentional about hurting your husband. He does have feelings. Men have feelings. Most times, they display them differently than women but they are there. Use your words as an opportunity to unlock the spaces of your husband's heart that wants to share with you, trust you, and bear with you how he feels. He is human first. Despite what he shows, he feels you through the words you speak. Be conscious of what feelings you're feeding him and feeding your marriage. Your words have power.

Be Intentional In Repair

After an argument couples might end up pillow talking in the bedroom. But it's what happens after the pillow talk that truly makes things last. If agreements were made on communication mechanics, roles, and responsibilities, or the like, keep your word to whatever next steps entail. Sex is good. It's wonderful and belongs in marriage. Enjoy the makeup sex, after sex, before sex, morning, noon, and evening sex. Have sex a lot! However, be sure that sex doesn't distract you both away from the goals that were set forth to keep the relationship on track. In repair mode, considering all else, be sensitive to what keeps each other accountable.

You can't be afraid of conflict or what the result of conflict will be. It won't be divorce if you don't want it to be. War and conflict are not synonymous with a negative loss. God allows things to surface when it will be for the marriage's greater benefit. Which doesn't take away the fact that the transition of growth might be uncomfortable. When God reveals how much work you have to do within yourself alongside or through the voice of your husband, it can feel like the sky is falling, the world is ending, and your relationship is about to fall off of a cliff. As women, we can be very imaginative in our thinking, at times even dramatic. Nonetheless, those feelings can overtake you and be very real and very present in your life and in your marriage. This place of insecurity exposed is the exact place God wants you. God wants you humble in order to recognize that change is not all about what your husband is doing, not doing or will do. It's about what you need to to do to please God. Confession of your transgressions will win the heart of your husband but obedience, even in conflict, pleases God and helps you win in the war for your marriage.

Winning wars happen when the fight is fought in unison to the leader's direction. You have to agree with God in face of your situation whether it looks contrary to what you believe is right or to what you know God promised. Follow God's lead even when your marriage doesn't look like or align with the standard of love. Get the help you need from the Lord in prayer. You must agree with God, connect with His promise, and the war on behalf of your marriage. He knows what, why, and when you both will pull through. The activities that follow this spiritual obedience sounds the alarm for your participation in warfare.

Declaring war through warfare is often a physical manifestation of a spiritual infiltration of hope, help, and transformation in a dark time. That's what makes the fight so hard. It's dark. It is difficult to see in the dark but the darkness has no bearing on your hearing. In the dark night of war, God will instruct you to praise, expect, believe, and speak like something good is about to happen, in a place when everything bad is going on in your relationship. Here's why. Warring on behalf of your marriage isn't just saying a prayer. "Just saying a prayer," isn't going to move strongholds, break curses, or release demonic attachments from your relationship. When you enter into spiritual warfare it must be perpetual. You can't stop until the war has been won. Yes, it will be hard. But you keep praying for your husband's safety and cooking your husband dinner even while you're at odds. There is nowhere in the Bible that says you have permission to cease your wifely responsibilities on account of conflict. No, ma'am! Slap that food on his plate if you have to or serve it to him cold if you need to, but don't stop doing what you are called to do, say, and be as a wife. Even in conflict, you are still his wife.

The position of prayer as a wife is strategic. It is creatively effective. It is in these uncomfortable positions of prayer that shift you into a posture of warfare. When I first went to war for my marriage, it was while we were homeless living at a scattered site. I prayed over my husband every day before I went to work. My mentor, Kecia, had given me special holy oil from her Missions trip to Israel. I used it faithfully although my husband hated the smell. I didn't know he hated the smell until I went to lay hands on his head one morning. As I smeared the oil across his forehead with my eyes closed, praying deeply in prayer, he grabbed my hand. I jumped and popped my eyes open stricken by the fear of being caught. I felt like I was in a scene from a scary movie and the monster found out where I was hiding. He told me not to put that stuff on his head anymore. We laugh now, but at the time I was devastated. I went to work perplexed because I knew God told me to pray over him during that time. I knew I was instructed to war on behalf of my husband, our marriage, and our situation. I was committed to using the anointing oil to break the chains that were keeping our relationship and life from being everything I thought it was supposed to be.

By the time I got home from work it was time for me to cook dinner. I made fried chicken, rice, and vegetables that night. I'll never forget it. While I fried up the chicken, I got the idea to add a little anointing oil to the grease. I prayed and sang while I cooked that day, adding drops of holy oil in-between songs. My husband tore that chicken up! He kept telling me how good it was. I laughed and kept asking him if he wanted more. He had at least three helpings. Per my husband, it was the best fried chicken he'd ever tasted. He had no idea how right he was. The chicken was definitely made extra special. A few weeks later we moved from the scattered site to an apartment which ended that particular season of warfare. God answered my prayers according to the measure of my faith.

Always remember, warfare coupled with prayer, can be as simple as a touch. It can be as simple as a smile or it can be in the oil of fried chicken grease! It's anywhere and everywhere God wants you, through it, to be. In warfare for your husband and your marriage, your instruction is always to move as He directs. No matter how crossed you feel about your husband or about how things are going or not going, go to war. Put your hope in God. He is in full control of your life and will keep His hand on your husband, on your marriage, and on your children. Let your warfare sound as loud, crazy, and wild as your faith in

God to shift your marriage to the next dimension. For this level of mountain moving power requires you to war for your marriage like never before. If you've done it before, when you go to war for your marriage this time, go with the intent to win.

Chapter 8

Control Freak

"You might change before he does."

God's timing is relevant. It is divine and may be hard to understand at a moment when you're hoping for and expecting change to occur in your marriage. I remember a time of calling out to God in prayer. With my pressing need, I prayed hard. I went all the way in, tears, tongues, you name it! When I came up from prayer, my husband and I got into an argument. I went back to

God questioning how this could even be possible. I just prayed. What happened? Why weren't things different? Did I not believe enough? Did I say the wrong thing? Why is he still the same? What I learned later was that things were different. Not in the way I was looking for, but things had changed. The reason I couldn't see the change was because I had control issues.

I never wanted to control my husband. Anyone who knows my husband, also knows how impossible of a notion that would be. He's not controllable. It's one of the things I love about him. He's free to be himself. At the time, I wasn't as free. I was in need of control and tried my best to control the situation. In my best stitch effort, I scrambled for stability. Due to my own experiences, I couldn't handle instability. It made me anxious. I needed everything to be perfect. Whenever things seemed to have fallen out of my grasp, I clambered for control. I clung to it for balance. Today, I know where my help comes from. However, back then, I was still learning how to trust God. I knew scripture, what to say and what words to use in prayer because I grew up in church. But I still had a lot of growing to do. One of the areas that needed to be strengthened was the area of trust. In this particular moment, I let my fear of losing control replace my faith in trusting God to take care of me and the situation that had gone haywire in my relationship. The truth is God always had it. He never left me, even when I didn't yet know how to trust Him.

There is a fine line between, control, demand, and expectations of which the remedy is confidence. As a praying wife, confidence is a position. It is an attitude. It is a poised state of mind that believes God will do exactly what He said He would do. It speaks as if the promise is present, right in front of her eyes. It joins together action and understanding and has peace about its hope. It is intentional. A confident wife lives as if the promise of change has already occurred. She sees her husband as a king, even before he acts like one. She has a sharp focus and the courage to be, do, and love, despite any fear. She has the courage to trust in God without limitations because He is the source of her strength and has proven repeatedly that He is trustworthy to keep any promise given. By nature, the new air of confidence will be noticeable to others who might perceive you as crazy. These people, friends, family, or foe, may find your confidence questionable. When a praying wife is confident, trusting that her marriage will thrive no matter what, the devil himself can feel it and shakes in his boots. However, her battle is never with Satan or his cohorts. Through prayer, she lets the Lord fight for her. A wife who trusts the Lord doesn't get in his way. She is a force to be reckoned.

Controlling

Controlling behavior communicates a lack of trust. It damages the intimacy in your marriage and gets in the way of God's work. Yes, honey. Your seizure for control is blocking the blessing you are looking for in your marriage. More often than most would care to admit, wives are blind to the damage being done when we try to control things in our relationship. We're blind because of our own fear and the overwhelming need to alleviate it. The longer your fear builds, the more difficult it will be to resolve later on. It becomes an idol. Realizing fear has become an idol in your life, prevents the marital success you truly desire. However, when you see it show up in your marriage you know its time to wake-up and consider change, a release of control and embracing trust in God. Returning your attention back to God can refocus your energy and restore your confidence in his ability to help you.

> "So do not fear, for I am with you; do
> not be dismayed, for I am your God.
> I will strengthen you and help you;
> I will uphold you with my righteous
> right hand."
>
> *Isaiah 41:10*

Demanding

When women demand or explode, men withdraw. Think about the last time you let your husband have it. You know, the time he had to pick his face up off of the floor. Remember the time you let him know what he could have, how he could have it, what to do with it and where he could put it? You delivered all of your fears, desires, frustrations, and released them in one gargantuan emotional explosion. While it was probably good that you finally got your true feelings out, how you got them out, through the explosion, ultimately won't serve to benefit either of you. In fact, your husband will feel like you've just created a whole lot of unnecessary drama and will check out. He might even completely withdraw emotionally or physically from the relationship. No matter how bad you needed that explosion, that result of him withdrawing is not what you expected the intended result to be.

Taking authority in alignment with prayer looks like a wife who is willing to listen, negotiate, and work through any issue that arises. It doesn't demand, it invites and exhibits the attributes of love; patience, kindness, and self-control. An explosion is a reflection of holding on to what needed to be said, for too long. No one hears an explosion, but everyone can feel it's effects. The aftermath of an emotionally demanding explosion can be devastating to a marriage and leave you both wishing you didn't say things you really didn't mean.

Expectation

Expectation is based on the idea of perfection, which is often embedded in fear. An unbalanced perception of expectation in a marriage focuses on the outcome of a situation so attentively, that as a result, a wife will feel an unhealthy pressure to create a specific outcome. The result forfeits being present for the journey of faith in getting there because expectation supports comfort zones. Faith blows those boundaries of comfortable expectation and fears out of the water. With faith, expectation looks for the good but is ok with the wait, the process, and the journey. To release unhealthy levels of control, demand, and expectation from your marriage means to submit your relationship to the feet of Jesus for healing.

"...As Jesus was getting into the boat, the man who had been demon-possessed begged to go with him. But Jesus said, "No, go home to your family, and tell them everything the Lord has done for you and how merciful he has been." So the man started off to visit the Ten Towns[c] of that region and began to proclaim the great things Jesus had done for him, and everyone was amazed at what he told them."

Mark 5:18-20

Beginning at the start of this chapter in Mark, you will find the full story of Jesus healing the demon-possessed man. What we can perceive from this verse highlights this man's family was completely done with him, the demons, and his behavior because when Jesus found him he was already living at the cemetery, and not with his family, familiar surroundings. Demon possessed or not, his family, circle of familiarity, disowned him because of his issue. The man was sick physically, mentally, and spiritually. He had issues only God could heal. Like your husband, God wants to heal you of the issues only He can see and only He knows about. In a marriage, there are times of change that require space for healing. Space can be explored on any level and as the relationship needs. The idea of space is challenging as a wife because it can make things feel shaky and unsure, not knowing if you and your husband are going to work out. There can even be just too many issues in the way to be able to see a positive end. But there is one. When you free yourself of the need to control the process, you'll begin to see it.

Freeing yourself from the need to have transformation happen in the order or the way you think it should, will bless your mind and give your heart and soul peace. Your mind is powerful and wired to believe whatever you think is possible. There are no limitations to God's ability and therefore should be no limitations on what you choose to believe about your husband and about your marriage. When you choose to believe good things about your marriage, good things will happen. You are supposed to believe that your husband's change will be real. You're supposed to see him in "new clothes." Even before he puts them on.

Marriage is forever. People change and grow at different paces. Relinquish the control to orchestrate the change you want to see in your marriage. Your strength as a wife is added to his strength as your husband when you connect to God in prayer. God wants to make you one, on a deeper level. It is his design. As a praying wife, God empowers you to bring great blessing to your husband through the use of your wifely influence. In most cases, the way God will invoke change through you won't look anything like what you want it to. But when God does moves in your marriage, you and your husband's lives will never be the same.

Chapter 9

Being Alone

"It's lonely here."

One of the perks of being married is knowing that you have someone who will have your back, no matter what, for a lifetime. However, either one of you can experience loneliness in the marriage. Yes, it sounds weird that you might feel alone and be married. But that's exactly the problem. Your husband is not designed and was not partnered with you to satisfy your loneliness.

Nor are you there to satisfy his in just being around. Your mission together is to build, to increase and multiply what you both put your hands to, including each other. Your marriage was never designed to be a setup for a permanent playdate. Your togetherness has an intended purpose. That being said, feeling alone and being alone in a marriage can mean two completely different things.

Feeling Alone

When loneliness hits, it distorts how you see your husband. It devalues your marital relationship. Loneliness is good for tricking you to believe your relationship is far less satisfying than it actually is. Loneliness is a strategy of disconnection. If the enemy can disconnect you from your husband, mentally, emotionally, and spiritually he can whisper anything in your ear and you'll believe it. Just like Eve, Satan wants to insulate you with isolation and ravage your marital thought life. He knows the power you have as your husband's wife. He knows the meaning of your support in actualizing the dreams, goals, and visions God placed inside of your husband. He knows, your husband needs you, and everything you bring to the table, in order for those dreams to manifest in the natural. Therefore if he can get you to be distracted by all of the ways your husband is unavailable to you, or if he can get you to be distracted by the guilt of having your own dreams and aspirations he wins in getting you off track to the mission of building. In the attack of loneliness, the enemy's goal is not only to disconnect you from your husband but slowly and assuredly, also from God. Because the further away you are from both, the more you'll listen and the deeper you will fall into dissatisfaction with your marriage until it is completely dissolved.

In a marriage, loneliness sounds like

transactional conversations about bills and responsibilities. It looks like daily routines that support emotional distance and losing affection daily. Ironically, you stay together, often out of a fear of being alone. Improving the quality of your relationship calls for intense marriage muscle strengthening. It will be a practice of patience and making a significant effort to reignite the value for each other as a married couple. Gaining a greater understanding of your husband's feelings will help you to show more understanding of him which invites intimacy back into the relationship. When intimacy is lost, loneliness will always be present.

Being Alone

Being alone is necessary. In your alone time away from what is familiar, such as your husband, family or friends, there is essentiality in replenishing you. It is the underlying foundation of which success for your marriage is built upon. To neglect it or lie to yourself about needing it adds cracks, in the form of stress, to your marital foundation. It takes away wholeness, the place you need to give your best self from, as a wife, in your relationship. It helps you focus on your own physical, mental, emotional, and spiritual needs.

In a position of alone time as a praying wife, don't use it as an opportunity to rebel. No, you cannot run away because alone time felt like pure bliss, it was supposed to. Yes, you have to return to the duties in your home. Your home needs you there. Rebellion shows it's ugly head in subtle ways and may be more present in your marriage than you think. I always thought of rebellion as something terribly not me. But it was. Especially in my marriage. When I began to heal from the devastation of sexual abuse from childhood, I started to find my voice. I didn't have one before. I was too busy holding too many secrets. My career supported finding my own voice. It helped me reach levels of success in a corporate job that I wouldn't have otherwise. I was a boss in every sense of the word. In the corporate setting, it was much easier to express my voice with boldness, authority, and conviction because there was no emotion required. Submissiveness was shunned. Success in this realm required no emotional engagement at all. Everything was black or white, it was or it wasn't. Very simple. It was perfect for me. However, when I got home, I was not the boss. I was a partner in a heart-centered relationship. A very different dynamic and one that I was still getting used to at the time. It took me years to realize and really hear my husband tell me I wasn't listening to him. In so many words he said I rebelled everything he said. He was right. I wasn't listening. I was too busy fighting for the heart of my voice I felt no one else wanted to hear from years past. Through years of prayer, practice, a few more arguments and lots of patience, I surrendered my rebellious, trying to be understood, heart to God. The more I asked God to show me how to share my voice in my marriage and really listen to my husband, the more I saw my husband's heart and could celebrate his leadership. And, the stronger we grew together as one. Rebellion rots away at the very foundation of marriage, destroys the union, and perverts God's purpose in your marriage, to build.

In your alone time with God, there are difficult things you can ask for. Things that when said aloud you feel embarrassed by. Things that when spoken from your lips you feel freed by. Things that when asked, will be done. With rested eyes, you will be sharp enough to see the signs, wonders, and miracles that are promised to follow when you believe what you're asking for is already done. In your alone time with God healing happens. Be bold. Don't be afraid. Be obedient. Be vulnerable. Surrender and be made whole. When you do, you will have power upon departing from your alone time. Let it shine in every area of your marriage. Embrace it but don't over exert it. Be wise with your power.

We forget the need to take care of ourselves more often then we should. As a wife, God needs you operating at your best self. Life may run you down and your marriage is the place where it will be felt first and most. Rejuvenate your being and refresh your mind by spending some alone time with yourself and with God. Chances are if you are feeling lonely, your husband is too. You both might feel an emotional disconnection. Find ways to either practice reconnecting with your husband or take advantage of times to be alone by yourself or with just each other. At the beginning and end of every day, the wholeness that you seek begins in prayer.

Chapter 10

Always Winning

"Wait, I thought I won?"

You can have victory in one area of your marriage and still have work to do in another. Overcoming one hurdle in a marriage only to find that there are others does not make your relationship any less powerful. It doesn't mean you've failed. It means you're alive, it means you're growing and most importantly it means you still need God's hand in your life and on your marriage.

Praying is a position of authority. Humble, knee-bowed, guard down, hands up in surrender, is the ready position of prayer. Nothing changes before you're ready. When you are ready for a change in your marriage you will win in prayer as a wife. To win in prayer for your marriage is to understand what you're really asking God to do. You may have thought you were asking for one thing but the reality is, that one thing, had multiple layers. When you only see one layer of that change manifest, you get discouraged. The question to challenge yourself with, is, do you even know what it is you're asking for? Whatever you ask God to do for your husband or for your marriage requires you to be ready to fulfill the other end. Meaning, in essence, you are a part of what you're praying for. If you pray for God to help your husband speak nicer to you, you're going to be called to forgive and speak nicer back to him. There is an instruction for every level of change your marriage will experience. Not just for your husband, but for you as well. Are you really ready for that? Are you ready to do everything it takes to be a part of the shift that will bring your marriage, your finances, your businesses, your children's prosperity, and your health to the next dimension? In some areas, you may be more than ready. That's good. But when you're experiencing dimensional shift you may not be as ready as you think you are. You may have to get ready for this new level of change God is calling your marriage to. Celebrate the victory of the war you won, but be open for the war to come, through prayer.

When you need a change real bad and desperation sets in, understand that begging is not praying. Begging God for change and calling it prayer devalues your authority as a wife who was given the power to speak life to every broken or dead thing in her marriage. What comes out of your mouth is based on what is inside your heart (Luke 6:45). If your heart is clouded with hurt, despair, and defeat, you will more than likely be speaking negative or death to yourself and your marriage. Cancel the negative noise you see, hear, and speak. It will be like cancer to the bones of your marriage. Brittle to a crumble will your negative words break down what is supposed to be built up, together. Be aware of the power of your words. Deal with those things that are negative so that what flows from your mouth about your husband and about your relationship is good and produces power. The ignition of power sets the stage for change. Let your mouth be a constant fountain of life (Proverbs 10:11). Look for opportunities to be kind and tender in heart toward your husband even after a major loss, even after a major win. There will always be more work to do. More battles to win, more victory to be lived. Nothing stays the same and thus you can't stop loving each other when times get tough or tougher.

God can't be "on the list," of things to have or remember concerning your marriage. He has to be your main priority, as a wife. As a couple. In trusting God, give yourself and your relationship permission to be free from the need of everything being perfect all of the time. It just won't be. However, God's grace is sufficient (2 Corinthians 12:9). Trust God's process of change, it's timing and the promise of peace that comes with it. Through prayer, change is never far from you. Actually, change is happening all around you because you've already won. You are a perpetual winner when God is the strength behind your fight.

A Call to Pray - War

In my authority as a wife,

I bind and blind the intentions of every evil

manifestation, temptation,

and exasperation of flesh from reaching

the eye gate, ear gate, and flesh gate of my

husband.

I cancel the plans, seen and unseen that are

set up to disrupt the will of God for our

marriage.

They will all spoil and decay opportunity for evil

and wickedness from flourishing over our

marriage.

They are depleted. Unhealthy attachments to

all people, places, and things are seared from

returning,

with the fire of the Holy Spirit.

Open the spiritual eyes of my husband to see any and everything that is rising itself up as evil against him. Give him the courage to tear it down with his words, choices and actions. Replenish the gaps of emptiness with fresh fire, anointing, and power from on high.

Fill my husband's heart with peace and conviction.
Block him from being swallowed up by the thrills of his imagination and fantasies of failure. Send your spirit of protection to cover his soul. Preserve his light, show him your way.
Give him your vision and direction so that together we may fulfill your purpose in our marriage.
Amen

AFTERWORD

The prayers in this book represent a place to begin praying for your husband. They do not resemble any formula for prayer or magic way to pray that will yield magic results. Through these prayers and your own, you are releasing the power of God's help to your marriage. God's power and presence are available to you through the confession of your own words. Effective fervent prayer has limited correlation to how long your prayer is or how many words you use in prayer. Yet has everything to do with your confession and how quickly you can believe God is able to do exceedingly, abundantly and above all you could ever ask or think, according to the power that works in you (Ephesians 3:20).

You see, prayer shifts the atmosphere. Believing in prayer shifts your heart toward God.

Staying in prayer shifts your marriage to a place of peace. You can't control what your husband does or does not do. But you can choose to respond differently through prayer. Aligned with gratitude and love, through prayer, you can learn to appreciate life for what it is, what it's not and what it will be. Letting go of everything familiar for the sake of change, for the sacrifice of love comes at a price that is uncomfortable. It will make you clutch your pearls for sure. However, being a wife whose prayers move mountains is about more than discomfort. It's about more than just saying nice things. It's a warring for your relational health, legacy, and prosperity.

Becoming a wife whose prayers move mountains is a shift in focus from problems to solutions. Or from trying to change each other to letting God do the dirty the work. It is taking care of your own emotional, physical and mental needs. It's keeping a journal, learning something new and dedicating time to self-preservation for the benefit of growth in the marriage. It is a respectful surrender to God that releases fear of loss, change, divorce, disappointment, loneliness, what other people think, what your husband will say, regret, the unknown, or even things staying the same. Knowing that you can trust God to handle any fear gives confidence to you as a wife who is committed to praying for her husband and her marriage.

The flow in becoming a wife whose prayers move mountains is boundless with healthy boundaries that celebrate the interconnection of intense love between each other. It is protected through the support of others when you just want to crawl under a rock because you're embarrassed, ashamed, or broken by the exposure of your marital issues. Having a strong support system outside of your marriage is vital to the success therein. It helps love to move uninhibitedly. Free of denial and self-doubt. It is curious for intimacy and speaks the truth in honesty and love. Willing to confront and heal the hardest and most difficult of circumstances.

Through my unconventional, amazingly non-traditional marriage, we learned that our best moments came from creating our life on our own, by our own terms. We literally drew a plan for our relationship back when we first started dating. Whenever we strayed from that, things were always chaotic. To you, I say get back to your own love. Draw the plan you see God giving to you both and execute it. Don't stray from it. Exhaust everything you have to offer each other and the world.

The sound of love is uniquely fierce. It echoes for an eternity. Let it. Let go even when it's hard. Forgive each other and move forward always. It sounds easy to do but it's not. It will take intentional thoughts, behaviors, words, and demonstrations. In this new season of winning in your marriage, disappointment and hurt can't be carried in. If you do, it will choke the blessing of peace, growth, and prosperity you and God desire for you both. You don't have time for that. Life is short. You only have time for love. Use love to create the opportunities that will help you build a legacy of praying and winning together as one.

Resources

Hopler, W. (2003). Find Peace and Confidence Despite a Difficult Marriage. Retrieved from: https://www.crosswalk.com/family/marriage/find-peace-and-confidence-despite-a-difficult-marriage-1220918.html

Groot, M.P., Kooke, R., Knoben, N., Vergeet, P., Keurentjes, J. J. B., Ouborg, N.J., & Verhoeven, K.J.F. (2016). Effects of Multi-Generational Stress Exposure and Offspring ENviornemnt ont he Expression and Perisstence of Transgenerational Effects in Arabidopsis thaliana. PLoS ONE, 11(3), e0151566.http://doi.org/10.1371/journal.pone.015166

McGibbon, E. & McPherson, C., (2013). Stress, Oppression & Women's Mental Health: A Discussion of the Health Consequences of Injustice. Women's Health and Urban Life, Vol 12 (2), 63-81.

Jacobs, J. (2009). All you need is love & other

lies about marriage. HarperCollins, New York, NY.

www.ingramcontent.com/pod-product-compliance
Lightning Source LLC
Chambersburg PA
CBHW061825040426
42447CB00012B/2815